I0472539

Adjuster's Life

From resume to payday

Douglas Lee Spurling

Table of Contents

Foreword

Ever dream of having the freedom to travel?

Do you ever wish you had more time off?

Adjuster's Life shows you how to do just that—and get paid for it to boot.

Your new business as an Independent Insurance Adjuster is at your fingertips. Begin today. Now there's no need to waste time and money going to an expensive school. What you need to know, from resume to payday, is packed inside the pages of this little book.

No sales gimmick or hook. Just the simple words of a seasoned adjuster penned with sweat from years of one on one field training.

This manual comes not only with words, examples and web-links, but a promise to personally coach as you build your adjusting career.

This business thrives in any economy, and you can too. Whether you're looking for a rewarding career or just want to become a better adjuster—this is for you.

Preface

My wife and I live a life of endless summers. We spend winters in Florida and summers on a lake in Minnesota. No—we're not retired. We're insurance adjusters. What you're about to read will show you how you can be one, too.

If I've heard it once I've heard it a thousand times. *How do I get a job like yours?* I'd always do my best to explain the details of Insurance Adjusting. If I could, I'd let them ride along. And after several days of bouncing around in my truck, standing on roofs sweating up a storm and listening to me carry on about what it takes to be an adjuster—they'd ride off into the sunset and become successful adjusters.

Before long more people wanted training than I could fit in my F250. Someone said: *You oughta write a book.*

And so, here you are.

Do you want to see what it's like to ride through a storm as an adjuster? Well then, what're you waiting for? Jump in—let's roll.

Introduction

In adjusting—and life—time is precious. I appreciate your investment of time and money in this book. I promise not waste either.

What you are about to read isn't fancy. It's raw, to the point, plain and simple; *this is how I do it* adjusting.

More than a book

Our goal is to help you become a successful adjuster. Thus, this book comes with the added benefit of a coach. While you're learning the ropes I welcome you to contact me with any questions during your journey. If you're like others I've trained, during the first stages of *runnin' & writin',* you'll have a myriad of questions...ask. If we can help we will—that's why we're here. dougspurling@aol.com.

To keep it simple this book reads like a novel. I start at the beginning, like you just jumped in the truck, and we ride through a storm clear to the end—to payday.

Chapter 1 ~ What's adjusting?

On my first deployment to a major hurricane I was a nervous green horn. I didn't have enough confidence to make a decision and so I asked questions—lots of them. That was good. Never be afraid to ask questions—lots of them. That's how you learn. And especially in the insurance world there is no dumb question. The policy language can be confusing and can be interpreted differently. So, if it's your first day on the job or you've been at it for thirty years—if you have a question—ask. And don't be ashamed to ask.

And don't worry, when you ask too many, and it's time to cut the umbilical cord they'll let you know. They did me. The long hours and endless flow of questions fired at my inside handler finally wore on his nerves until he blurted out:

You're an adjuster—adjust.

I continue to ask questions—lots of them. But, I don't think he realized the wisdom of his words that day. I've forgotten his name, but still remember his words. It remains some of the best advice I've been given regarding adjusting even after all these years.

You may do the same things over and over, but no claim should be considered a brainless cookie-cutter exercise.

Consider each and every claim as having its own unique set of circumstances and inspect each scenario against policy guidelines and then, make a recommendation accordingly. As an adjuster you're paid to make decisions and give recommendations.

Kind of like CSI

Sometimes the human element gets involved and things get a little hairy. You may hear someone tell you that old crack in the drywall resulted from a tree hitting the roof. Perhaps. Perhaps not. Your job is to gather evidence and determine what direct physical damage was related to the insured peril. And also, just as important—damage not related to the insured peril—especially damages claimed by insured as resultant damage. We'll get into that, in more detail later.

Remember, adjusting, in a nutshell is to let the carrier know if they need to write a check and if so; why, and how much.

You are the eyes and ears of the carrier. You are to see what happened. Listen to what the Insured said happened. And document this through photos, sketches and written word. Generally the carrier is the check writer, and they will hold the final decision regarding what gets paid. An official statement you can make might sound like this:

"I do not have authority to extend or deny coverage."

But, I usually say something like:

"It's not my check book, so your carrier will make the final decision. If it were my check book…I'd be fishing right now."

This statement basically says the same thing but in a way they'll remember—which keeps you off the hook, and are less likely to get confused and say you promised them a big fat check.

Background Training Prerequisite

The best background, in my opinion, is to have a basic knowledge of construction. After all you'll be writing estimates for repairs. If a tree knocks a hole through the roof, can you rebuild it on paper?

If you don't have any idea about construction that's an easy fix. Find any storm chasing roofing company and tell them you want to sell roofs for them. If you have a pulse they'll hire you—straight commission of course. Hang out for a storm or two and you'll be meeting with adjusters inspecting roofs for hail damage normally. You'll learn the basics of roof and siding measuring, installation and repairs. You'll have the opportunity to read the finished product of insurance claims from several different carriers and you'll meet lots of adjusters and you can pick their brains and learn insurance adjuster lingo.

And if you work hard you can make a good income while you learn. Many good adjusters started out as roofing salesman.

That is just one simple way to get your feet wet in the world of an adjuster. It's not necessary but a working knowledge of construction will assist you a great deal when it comes time to write an estimate for repairs from a chicken dinner gone wrong that burned half the kitchen down. But this is about becoming an adjuster, so I'm not going to delve into construction basics 101.

License

The first solid step toward actually becoming an adjuster is to become licensed. I'm asked often. How do I do what you do? Do I have to go to school? The answer is yes and no.

You don't have to go to school, but you do have to pass a test to obtain an adjuster's license for your state. However, some states do not require an adjuster's license. In that case if you live in Missouri for instance, you can adjust claims without an adjuster's license.

But, you'll be hard pressed to find anyone who will give you a claim to run if you don't have a license. So even though it's not required per se by law—it is required by the folks who'll give you the claims. So, by default, you're going to have to obtain an adjuster's license from somewhere.

The common consensus is that Texas is the easiest place to obtain a license. I've been licensed in multiple states and I didn't notice one being harder than the other once you figured out what they wanted. Some states are more user-friendly. They tell you exactly what to do in easy to follow steps. While other states like Minnesota, the last time I took a test for them, are not so user-friendly. They said you need to pass the test, but they didn't provide any easy access as to what information was on the test so you could prepare—I think they call that, Minnesota nice.

Anyway, if you live in a state that requires a license you'll need to get licensed as a resident adjuster for that state if you want to run claims in that state. You can go to http://catadjuster.org/Channels/Licensing.aspx to find out your state requirements for obtaining a license in your particular state.

You can go to school for a fee and obtain a license. Fees usually range anywhere from $300 - $700 and last a few days to a week. You can get a license anywhere even if you don't live there. If you live in Minnesota and want to get a license in Texas, you can. And many folks do this. You will be allowed to get a non-resident license. The Texas license is recognized or reciprocal in several other states. Thus, allowing you to work claims in other reciprocal states. So, you can have a Texas license, and then if a hurricane hits Mississippi, you can work claims there because you are licensed in Texas.

The individual states many times require you to purchase a temporary license or they may call it an emergency license. They'll charge the adjusters flooding their state a nominal fee usually $25-$45 for a license that is good for 90 days or so allowing you to work the storm. After that you can keep up the license simply by renewing it, which of course requires another fee. It's a source of revenue for the state and regulates in a small way who is in their state adjusting.

Remember, I said the answer was yes and no, regarding whether you had to go to school to be an adjuster. Well, the reason I said that was because of continuing education requirements. Typically every two years you must renew your license—pay a fee, of course—

and document that you have completed the required number of hours of continuing education.

The requirements vary from state to state. But generally around 20-30 hours. You can choose how you want to do this. A vacation to Florida to attend a three day training when it's 20 below zero in your hometown may be a nice way to fulfill your requirements and take a tax deductible vacation. Also, you can take online courses. Each state will advise individually what classes are required and acceptable as CE credits. Go here to see what your state requires: http://catadjuster.org/Channels/Licensing.aspx.

So, in summary go to the website for your particular state and read what is required for licensing procedures. Take the test. If you don't pass, don't feel bad—count it as training. One of the best adjusters I know took the test five times before he passed. So, take the test as many times as you need to and count all the ones prior to passing as practice exams. When you pass the test--smile and say, "I'm a licensed adjuster."

Yeehaw!

Now what?

Having a license doesn't make you any money. It doesn't give you any claims to run. And it doesn't teach you how to handle a claim even if you got one. Actually, getting licensed has little to do with the actual workings of how to be an adjuster.

But, never fear...that's why I'm here. ☺

Chapter 2 ~ Getting Started

This is the part where I can help you get rolling, keep rolling and enjoy it along the way. This book isn't written to teach you how to pass your test. Passing the test makes you licensed, but it doesn't make you an adjuster.

Getting claims, running them, writing them, turning them in, having them be accepted by the carrier, the insured and the contractor is what gets you paid and makes you an adjuster. In short you're an adjuster when you successfully and efficiently are closing claims. Or as they say in the field: *Turnin' & burnin'* or *Runnin' and writin'*

Let's get started.

Resume

Get your name out there. Not unlike any business you need to solicit if you want to get called. Write a resume heavy with any construction and estimate writing background. You want to show that you know what it takes to fix a damaged structure. Even if you don't know how to physically do the work, you need to be able to show what needs to be done on paper, in the form of an estimate, reflecting step by step repair procedures.

Let's say for example you receive a claim where a tree has damaged part of the insured's roof. You will need to know what needs to happen to make repairs and be able to communicate it on paper. Such as; replacing the tree damaged insulation, rafters, sheathing, felt, drip edge, shingles, fascia, soffit etc. Notice I listed in an order that resembles the actual layers of a roofing system. If you get in the habit of writing your estimates in a way that makes sense, it will help you to not forget anything, and it makes it easier for your file reviewer to understand your estimate.

If you are working a flood you may want to start at the pad and work your way up on your room by room estimate; pad, carpet, baseboard, drywall, paint... We'll go into more detail about this later.

For now let it suffice to say you want to impress anyone reading your resume that you know construction and you can write an estimate.

Secondly, if you have any knowledge at all of the Xactimate program you want to put the word *Xactimate* in your resume. It is the most popular adjuster's program. The carrier will dictate which program you use, and most likely it will be Xactimate. We'll talk about other programs later and by the time you finish this book I tell you how you'll at least be able to put on your resume that you have working knowledge of Xactimate and other adjuster software programs. The key here is to just have the word Xactimate on your resume. It'll help.

The next thing you want to show on the resume is people skills. Although technically your job is to determine cost of repairs for insured damages, really *you're in the people business*. And don't forget it. If you do—your life as an adjuster will be miserable. You need to do all of this in a way that makes everybody happy—as much as possible. You want to show that you're able to communicate well with others. You're the face of the insurance company—their representative. They want to know you will represent them well.

In summary your resume should show that you have knowledge of construction, estimate writing, the word Xactimate, and you're good with people.

Go to http://catadjuster.org/ Scroll down and find the heading, Resume hosting, on the right margin. It states:

> Adjusters we provide a free resume hosting service. Just create a free account, login and visit the Roster to add your information and upload your resume. The Roster is used by many employers to locate adjusters so don't miss out on an opportunity add your name to the National Adjuster Roster.

Jump through the hoops and get your name listed on their roster as a licensed adjuster ready to be deployed. Then turn your ringer up and listen for the phone. While you're waiting be sure to finish this book, so you'll know what to do when the phone rings.

Also while you're at CADO (Cat Adjuster Dot Org.) click on the 'Classifieds' tab. It's located on the top second from the left. Then click on jobs. You'll notice venders looking for adjusters.

A vender is like an employment agency for adjusters. A carrier is the insurance company. Click on any vender looking for adjusters and send them your resume. You may need to fill out their online application to be officially on their roster. Getting on a roster is simply getting your name on their list of adjusters. Get on as many rosters as you can for starters. Of course, you can't deploy for more than one vender but until you get your foot in the door and have more work than you can handle—get your name on every roster out there.

As I write this a hurricane is threatening the east coast. I am being contacted by venders requesting I go on standby in the event the 'cane makes landfall. The CADO website is full of venders asking for adjusters to go on their roster.

You see, a vender wants bragging rights to the carrier. So, the more adjusters they have on their roster the more they can tell the carrier they can handle.

The carrier (insurance company) can make one phone call to a vender (adjusting company) and say we need a thousand adjusters on the east coast. The vender puts out a deployment request to the adjusters on their roster.

In catastrophes with advance knowledge, like a hurricane, the vender will put adjusters willing to deploy on standby. Which means: be packed, have the truck full of fuel, and if we confirm be ready to roll.

Speaking of which...will you please excuse me—I gotta go

I'm back—miss me?

I just took a six week break from writing this—got deployed. Hurricane Sandy, I mean, Super Storm Sandy. I think the governor changed her name so the carriers couldn't apply the hurricane deductible—wasn't that nice? Wonder if that got him any votes.

I worked in-house this time rather than going to the field to fight the cold and snow. We were paid $400 per day. Once you gain enough experience you can opt to work inside as a file reviewer. Typically you'll work twelve hour days—from seven to seven, six or seven days a week at a storm office. You will be examining the claims sent in by field adjusters for quality control. It's a good gig usually for the old dogs that'd rather lie on the porch and bark rather than go out and run the field. A field adjuster can make twice as much, but he works twice as hard, too.

Anyway, where were we?

Oh, yeah...

CHAPTER 3 ~ Deployed!

You may hear nothing for months and think you're forgotten and then a hurricane shows up on the radar and suddenly you'll feel like the most popular guy in town. Phone calls and e-mails will start pouring in and all of a sudden you're in high demand.

You will need to make a decision and pick which vender you want to work for, and go on standby with that one. Contact all the others and thank them for thinking of you and request they keep you on their roster, however, this time you're already on standby. This way you don't burn bridges. Eventually, if you do a good job, you'll be on the top of the list for your favorite vender and you won't be concerned about being on other rosters. But never burn a bridge.

Getting deployed is exciting and you'll think it's a dream come true. But, that dream can turn into a nightmare pretty quick if you're not prepared. It's important to know before you go. It can be a long time between paychecks and an expensive road trip if you aren't ready to *turn and burn* when you hit the storm site. But, never fear—that's why I'm here.

Okay. So, you've passed the test, got your license, posted your resume and now you're on your way to, Hurricane Virgin. What should you do?

There are various idiosyncrasies depending on which vender you are deployed with and which carrier you're representing. Sometimes you'll be working with one vender but handling claims for different carriers. This makes it a little more confusing because, different strokes for different folks.

Basically you will be doing the same thing for everyone, but saying it in a way to suit the carrier. In other words, you're going to be doing the same thing no matter who you work for, but one company may want you to, two-step while another wants you to waltz—either way you're dancing, it's just to their music.

And since they are paying you to visit their insured and handle their claim, they have the right to determine how they want you to dance. No matter what kind of music they play or what language they want you to say it in, just remember at the end of the day, the carrier wants to know three things:

1) Do we owe?
2) Why or why not.
3) If so—how much.

And they want you to tell them five different ways:

1) Tell them with words
2) Tell them with photos
3) Tell them with diagrams
4) Tell them with an estimate
5) Tell them your bill $:-)

We'll cover how to tell them soon.

Remember, never be afraid to ask questions. The vender makes money when you make money, so if you have a question—ask. Odds are if you have a question others have the same question too.

NOTE: Some adjusters will work for more than one vender. You can do this because you're an independent contractor. I worked for three venders at one time and it about drove me crazy trying to keep straight how each one wanted their claims packaged, and

I just got plumb wore out. Furthermore, if you run too thin, you're not doing the best you can for any one.

I recommend you do a great job for one, rather than a mediocre job for several. Even if you have a lull in the action occasionally, I think being loyal to one vender, will pay off in the long run—but that's a decision you have to make since I don't have your energy, or pay your bills.

Take your time—you'll get there faster...because, time is one of your a most valuable assets.

Setting up your claims

You finally get to your hotel. You drove all night and you're tired and nervous. You plop down on the bed and open your lap top. You're happy to see a claim has been e-mailed to you. But within a few minutes you're petrified to see a hundred claims have been e-mailed to you. You start to read the first claim loss report and notice the guidelines tell you that you must make twenty-four hour contact and inspect within seventy-two hours.

Now, you might feel overwhelmed. How am I going to run all these claims in three days? *Take your time—you'll get there faster*. That's one of my *Dougism's*. I think I've said it to every adjuster I've ever trained in. On the surface it may sound like it doesn't make sense, but in practice it works, especially when time is an issue. And when you're working a storm your most precious commodity is time. Learn to use it well and you'll calm the storm.

Typical protocol for claims handling applies at all times, whenever possible. At a CAT (catastrophe) it's not possible. So, you're an adjuster—adjust.

A hundred claims in a hundred different places. Where do you begin?

You should get the claims printed. Technology is changing every second. I used to haul a printer with me and print the claims. Now, I've adapted a process to save time and money. You don't have to do it the way I do, and you may discover a better way, but this is what I've found to work well and efficient.

The key is to do it like McDonald's. Do the same thing every time. And then, if it's one or one hundred and one claims you can handle it, because it's just one claim— you just do it over and over.

Here's what I do when I have a hundred claims in my e-mail inbox.

I have three things open on my desktop: a new Word doc., a mapping program, and my e-mail.

The first thing that needs to happen is that I need to get claims printed, mapped and phone calls made with appointment times. This you should attempt to do within twenty-four hours of receiving the claim.

- Print
- Map

- Call

I open the first claim and highlight and copy only what I need; which is the name of carrier (Insurance Company). You may think you don't need this but if you start working more than one carrier you'll be glad you have it when a cautious insured asks you who you're with. If you say State Farm when you should have said All State—you won't be in good hands.

You'll also need the claim number, they ask for that a lot to prove you're who you say you are. And then, of course you need the insured's name, address, phone number and a brief description of damage.

You may need policy information depending on the type of loss. For example if your claim is a commercial or farm policy and you're looking at several buildings you'll want to know if that structure is covered, for how much and what type of coverage, ACV (actual cash value) or RCV (replacement cost). The loss report may have several pages but generally all you need is how to reach the folks and what they're claiming.

So in summary, what you want to copy from the loss report to a claim sheet is:

- Carrier (Insurance Company)
- Claim number
- Insured's name, address, contact information
- Description of damage
- Coverage info. (possibly)

I paste the information from the e-mail to the empty Word doc. This will become your claim sheet, or field report or whatever you want to call it. It will be what you take notes on during your inspection.

Then I highlight and copy the address and I paste it into a mapping program. Choose whatever one you like as long as it can accept numerous addresses at one time, such as Streets and Trips, DeLorme or Map Quest.

I highlight the insured's name and save the Word doc to their name. I create a folder on my desk top named after the storm, for example: Hurricane Virgin or 2012 Ice. This way you'll have a simple record of every claim separated by catastrophes. Repeat this until you have every claim copied to a Word document, and the addresses input on your mapping program. And you didn't have to type anything—just copy and paste.

Printing—without a printer

Next to print the claims without a printer. I have an account with efax; http://www.efax.com/. You can send and receive faxes from your computer similar to sending an e-mail. I fax the claims in one fax from the folder on my desktop to the front desk of the hotel.

Which reminds me, of a side note here: I try to stay in the same hotel chain, Choice Hotels. As a member you gather points toward free stays and I'm not charged for my faxes.

Appointment Setting

While I'm waiting for a call from the front desk to let me know I have a fax, I look at the map to decide what order to run the claims. Whatever makes the most sense geographically is how you try to run them.

Once I get the claims I put them in the order I'd like to run them. I put the appointment time and date in the top right hand corner. For example: Mon. 10.22.12. 9-10 a.m. I give myself an hour window for time of arrival. Set as many claims per day as you can run and write. This will vary depending on the type of claims you're running. Leave yourself enough time so you're not rushed. Four to five claims per day is a good number.

When I was younger I'd run eight or more a day as long as it was light enough to take pictures I was running. But ultimately what would happen is, I'd get behind on my paper work and I'd have to take off a few days or more, to write.

It may sound like a good plan until implemented. The trouble with running as many as possible and then stopping to write is that the first claims are old by the time you get them submitted and the folks will begin calling asking, *where's my money?*

The quality of your work suffers as well with the passage of time before writing your claim.

Imagine writing an estimate, labeling photos and summarizing your conversation with the insured within a day of your inspection. The inspection is still fresh in your mind.

Now, let's say a week has gone by and you've taken a thousand photos, you've looked at thirty houses and have had as many conversations with homeowners and contractors. Now, you're trying to remember thirty houses ago, one thousand photos ago and sixty conversations ago to write your estimate. As good of a memory as you may have, and as good of notes as you may take, in the long run it'll take you longer to do it this way—and you won't produce as good of quality loss report.

I run six days per week. If you have claims with interior damage sometimes they are best run on Saturdays because folks are home more often that day.

An example of a time schedule is:

Arrive at first claim between 9-10:00 a.m.

Arrive at second claim between 11-12:00 p.m.

Third claim 1-2:00 p.m.

Fourth claim 2-3:00 p.m.

Fifth claim 3-4:00 p.m.

CHAPTER 4 ~ Initial Contact

It's important to contact your insured's within twenty four hours of receiving the claim. Give them your name and phone number and the time you'd like to run the claim. You don't want the insured making phone calls wondering why they haven't heard from their adjuster.

If you can't get your appointments figured out within the first twenty-four hours, still make your initial contacts. Just advise insured that you've been assigned as their adjuster and you're giving them a courtesy call. Give them your name and phone number. Let them know you'll be calling back in a day or two with an appointment time. If you get the feeling they're impatient ask them if a certain day or time is better for them than another, and then let them know you'll do your best to accommodate them. That should buy you some time to get your schedule figured out.

It saves a lot of time to set your appointment during your initial contact. If you get an answering machine leave the same information, name, phone number and anticipated time of arrival. Make sure you note that you lmom (left message on machine).

The words you say are important during your first contact. Your first contact sets the stage for the rest of the claim process. In many ways the insured may view you as their only hope. You're their Hurricane Hero; their Christmas in July, Santa-Send-Me-Money. So you've got to watch everything you say, because they're listening.

Hi, my name is Super Adjuster. I've been assigned to handle the insurance claim for hail damage filed by Insured Joe Schmoe.

This tells them immediately who you are and why you've called. It will avoid hang-ups from folks that may think you're a salesman.

You should avoid asking up front, "Is this Joe Schmoe?" It wastes time and in my opinion, it's rude and puts folks on the defensive—they don't want to tell some stranger calling out of the blue who they are. First impressions are powerful—make yours a good one. Introduce yourself first.

Also don't say, "This is Super Adjuster with ABC Insurance Co." Technically, an independent adjuster is not 'with' the insurance carrier. They are independent contractors representing the carrier. So, saying you've been assigned to handle the claim for ABC Insurance Company helps the carriers distance themselves from liability if the adjuster says or does something amiss or makes promises the carrier is unwilling to keep. NOTE: It's rare but certain carriers may request you say you're 'with' them—in that case, disregard what I just said.

I say something like this:

"Hi this is Doug Spurling, I've been assigned to handle the insurance claim for hail damage filed by Joe Schmoe; can I speak with him?"

"Sure, hold on"

"Hello, this is Joe"

"Hi, Mr Schmoe, this is Doug Spurling, I've been assigned to handle your hail damage claim. How are you?"

I always say, "How are you," and stop. I give them a chance to vent if necessary—which often is the case in bad storms like hurricanes, floods or tornadoes. Not so much in a hail storm. This question sets the insured at ease. If I'm willing to take my time at the beginning, it'll save me time in the long run. I want them to know, I'm on their side.

Too many people think that dealing with an insurance company is a battle. You want them to know right up front, that you're there to help. You see, they may already be on the defense.

They may have been told they need to watch out for the big bad insurance company or they'll get ripped off. They may have been told that they need representation by a public adjuster or contractor or lawyer or neighbor or otherwise they'll never get what they've got coming.

None of which is true, but if they believe it, you may have a difficult time getting the insured to cooperate, and it may cause problems setting your appointment right out of the gate, all because they come out with their dukes up, thinking you're going to show up swinging.

So, set them at ease and take the time to listen to their story. That'll save you a lot of time in the long run. Get them heading in your direction by letting them know you want to help. Taking the time to set the direction and momentum will generally carry you smoothly through the entire claim process.

While they're talking, make notes of any concerns they bring up, even trivial ones. If they mention the wood fence or deck, you had better make a note and make sure you take photos and document those items as well. If you forget to mention them, because you don't see any damage, it'll come back to haunt you when it's not on your report.

Most of the time you'll answer their initial questions regarding the loss with the same answer:

> *"Thanks for telling me about that, I've noted it so I'll be sure to take a look at it when I get there. You can remind me too, to make sure I don't forget, OK?"*

Develop a spirit of cooperation right off the bat. You're working with, not against, them.

You can't adjust the claim over the phone so don't try. They may try to get you to commit to coverage before you show up—don't. You can't see it. In the same regard remember you can't deny coverage over the phone, either. You have to see it to give every opportunity to find coverage.

NOTE: generally speaking an adjuster doesn't have authority to extend or deny coverage.

The insured may ask if they can remove items already damaged. This is tricky, because if you say, *sure throw it out*, and then find out that it wasn't damaged under a covered peril—you're on thin ice. If you say, *no, and the loss gets worse by waiting—like a water loss that grows mold, or a tree limb that's crushes the home –* you're on thin ice.

So, I'll ask, *"If there was no such thing as insurance—would you throw it out?"*

Good old fashioned horse sense goes a long way. If the rugs on fire, you don't wait to find out if insurance will cover it—you throw it out so the rest of the house doesn't burn down...right? No brainer. Use the same type of logic. Sometimes when money gets involved common sense gets muddled.

Now, if you want your insurance company to pay for the rug you threw out, you'll have to save the rug, or be able to give good photo documentation; and, if it's expensive, verifiable evidence of its value, such as a receipt.

Common sense—right?

I know the above mentioned example was over simplified, but in theory that's a good way to look at the claim from the vantage point of your initial contact. You can't get too deep regarding coverage issues at this initial stage of the claim process. If you do, you'll waste a lot of time and may dig a hole hard to get out of, once you finally arrive at the loss site.

It's important to let the insured know the following:

- They have a responsibility to protect their insured property from further damages regardless of coverage.

- They should try to provide photo documentation of any repairs or mitigation. For example: take photos of water damaged carpet, pad, drywall, personal property etc. before removal

- If insured is going to dispose of floor-covering ask them to save a sample (eight or twelve inch square is fine—you may have to mail it, so if it's too big you'll have to cut it to fit in the mailer)

- If insured has personal property damage, make sure to tell them not to discard it prior to your inspection, unless they can provide good photo documentation of the damaged items. Also ask them to make a list of damaged items with description, age and cost. Any electronic or appliance type items should include make, model and serial numbers.

- Remember you do not have authority to extend or deny coverage—especially over the phone during your initial contact.

Remember, this is just your initial contact and your goal is to get an appointment set. Rabbit trailing in conversations will gobble up valuable time and won't get anywhere. Let them talk, but your answers need to be limited and focused.

Now, close the deal.

"I've been making my schedule and I'll be in your area on Tuesday afternoon. It looks like I should be able to get to your place sometime between 1 & 2:00. I can't say exactly when I'll get there because I never know how long each claim is

going to take. Would that be alright if I swing by?"

You say you should be able to arrive somewhere between 1 & 2:00, but what they hear is: You'll be at their house from 1-2:00. So, if you add the second statement about not being able to say exactly when you can get there because you never know how long each claim is going to take—then some of them will understand and you won't get a phone call from the office telling you that your insured called, mad because you never showed up and never called to let them know you were going to be late, and you look at the time and it's 1:05. Sounds crazy but it happens.

If you are running late and won't get there within your hour window, call. If you are running late and won't get there within your hour window, call. Did I mention that if you're gonna be late – even if it's going to be close to the back side of your target time of arrival, CALL. The courtesy will go a long way, and it'll save you a lot of grief.

If you have trouble getting the appointment set because insured says they're not going to be home. You can follow up by saying something like this: (If all damages are exterior and your carrier allows it.)

"I understand and that's fine, it happens a lot. Many times folks aren't home when I inspect because they have to work. But I still inspect if all the damage is on the exterior. I just like to get you permission to stop by, so I don't get shot at from the neighbors or something."

That usually loosens them up, and they'll give you permission to inspect without them being home. But, sometimes they'll say, "Well, I need to show you the damage so you don't miss anything."

You want to say, "Listen here, I do this for a living and I can probably find more than you with my eyes closed. I don't need your help." But don't say that. Instead say something like:

"Oh, that'd be great if you could, hmmm, let's see, I'm not sure yet when I'll be back in that area. I know, how about you make a list for me to go through all the damage you've found? You can leave it in your door or something for me and I can use it to help me during my inspection. And then if it's OK with you, I could call you from your property if I have any questions. What do you think about that?"

Usually, that will give you permission to inspect with them not being there. Make sure you note that you're inspecting with permission.

You can keep in mind—but don't force the issue—by claim filing the insured has requested an inspection. But don't rub their nose in it and try to force the appointment. If you do you'll just create a confrontational environment and nothing good will come of it.

Remember, they are the customer so you must be cordial, but you're not a salesman that accommodates any time frame just to get an appointment. You are more like a repairman—and they need something fixed. You're letting them know when you can stop by to diagnose the problem. Get it?

Another thing you'll hear a lot is: "My contractor said he wants to be here during your inspection." When you hear that, say something like this:

> *"That's great, I know a lot of them like to be present for our inspection, and I allow that—it's OK with me—of course, that is, as long as they can accommodate my schedule and be there when I'm available. Of course you understand I'm unable to have 300 contractors controlling my schedule."*

They may want you to call the contractor to set the appointment, and you can if you want. If you're really busy you may just tell them:

> *"I don't mind if you tell your contractor what time I'll be there, he's welcome to join me. You can even give him my cell phone number, so he can call if he wants."*

You cannot possibly call every contractor and try to jive your calendar with theirs. (Well, maybe it would be possible—but why would you want to use up your precious time doing it?)

Most generally if you handle your appointment setting as described above you'll be able to set your appointments in the order you want.

Sometimes you just can't no matter how hard you try. In that case the insured's claim gets put to the bottom of the pile, and you set them up when your schedule allows and you're back in the area. Make sure you document your conversation and time and date you attempted to make inspection. Get a firm appointment set as soon as possible, even if it's set for a week or more out. Document the file by sending a note to your vender and or carrier, so they don't think you dropped the ball when this claim starts to age.

NOTE: Sometimes a claim must be inserted and screw-up your otherwise perfect schedule. It happens because the claim is high priority. It becomes high priority, because the damage is severe, or potentially severe like water loss with potential mold issues or fire or collapse or sometimes it's not the severity of the damage but the severity of the insured's impatient attitude. Some folks just need to be handled differently. And remember, you're in the people business. You'll learn that sometimes the ones that scream the loudest are the ones that have the least amount of damage.

I remember working a hurricane some years ago and while I was setting an appointment with an insured she said, "Don't worry about me sonny, other people need you more than I do. Whenever you can get here is fine with me." And so, I worked her in when it fit into our schedule the best.

I'll never forget pulling up to her two-story home. A tree the size of a telephone pole was sticking out of her roof like a javelin. As calm as Sunday afternoon tea, this sweet little southern lady answered the door and led me up to her room. When she opened the door a cool autumn wind hit me like I was standing outside. A sixteen inch diameter tree was perched on the bed and extended out the ceiling of the room exposing the clear sky above. She said, "It was no bother, I just shut the door."

I said, "I'm sure glad no one was lying on that bed when the tree hit."

She just smiled and waved her thin little hand, "I was sleeping in that bed, but it didn't touch me, praise the Lord. And I have another bed to sleep in."

And then, I've had others... you'd think the house was still on fire. You couldn't get there fast enough to suit them, only to find out the damage was so minor if they didn't point it out you'd have missed it.

Once I get the appointment confirmed I write *confirmed* on the top and circle it. If I only get the answering machine I write *LMOM (left message on machine)*.

Remember; filing a claim is a request by the insured to allow an inspection by an insurance adjuster. They have made the request for an inspection—period. You have been invited. It is in your best interest to be as accommodating and courteous as possible, and at the same time maintain control by not allowing the insured or contractor to hijack your schedule by dictating when you set your appointments.

CHAPTER 5 ~ Setting up files

I keep everything simple. I can run a hurricane with hundreds of claims with some paper clips and a few simple folders, that vanilla kind (or is it manila?).

Remember, it's like McDonald's making Big Macs—they can make one or one billion—they just do the same thing every time. You can run one claim or a hundred and one; if you do the same thing every time, you'll have a much more harmonious outcome, and you won't get burned out along the way.

The same holds true with big claims or small claims. If you get into the routine of doing the same thing each time—then you'll be able to work a claim worth a few hundred bucks and one for a few hundred thousand with ease.

Remember...

They're all easy—some just take longer than others.

After all the calls are made and after I've written the day, date and time of each appointment in the top right hand corner of each claim sheet I paper clip them together by days. For example all Monday 10.22.12 is paper clipped together, then Tuesday 10.23.12 and so on.

Then, I take three manila envelopes and label one *RUN,* another, *WRITE* and the other, *S2C* (Sent to close). I place all the claims in the *RUN* folder and after they're *run,* they are switched to the *write* folder and then once they're written and sent to close they are—you guessed it—sent to the *S2C* folder.

If I get buried and new claims are coming in faster than I can set appointments for right away, I make another folder which I label *SET*. All the new claims get thrown in there until I can get them mapped and called and appointments set. When I do, then of course they are transferred to the *RUN* folder.

Folders:

- RUN
- WRITE
- S2C
- SET (if necessary)

Time is your most precious commodity in this business, and in life for that matter, so pay special attention to using your time wisely.

Remember...

Take your time—you'll get there faster.

Document. Document. Document.

You're in the people business.

Now, before you go to sleep make sure your camera is ready. Which means your memory stick is empty and your batteries are being charged. You don't want to scale roof Mount Everest and start to take your roof overview photo and realize your batteries are dead. It stinks—I know. And you don't want to get half way through your day and realize you filled your memory stick.

Speaking of which, make sure your camera/memory stick can hold around 300 pictures. I'll get into more detail when we talk about tools of the trade.

Okay, call home, tell your family you love and miss them, say your prayers and get a good night's rest cause tomorrow it's SHOW TIME.

CHAPTER 6 ~ Show Time - The Inspection

Finally, you're two dozen pages in and haven't even rung the door bell. Well, now's your chance.

You've found their house—make sure it's their house. Don't be like me and find out after you've spent an hour inspecting a black roof in sweltering heat that there's two Rodriguez's and one lives at 2208 Shauna Lane (the one you inspected) and the other (your insured) lives one block over on 2208 Shauna Street. Kansas City is tricky like that. Trust me—I know.

You pull up to the house, double check you're at the correct address—did I already mention that. Triple check you're at the correct address. Snooping around the wrong address could also get you shot—but that's another story.

Before I get out of the truck I write on the claim sheet (the one you printed in the hotel with the name address etc.) F= ___ and then I put N or S or E or W (north, south, east or west) depending which way the front is facing. I also make a note, while still sitting in the truck, about the characteristics of the house; 2STRY/V/ARCH 8-10.That tells me the risk (insured's property) is a two story with vinyl siding and an architectural roof about 8-10 years old.

Later when writing your report you'll need this information, so it saves time to make a note right up front rather than having to look back at your photos because you can't remember.

Generally speaking in the adjusting world, the left side of the house is your left when you stand in the street looking at the front of the house. I like to label the elevations (sides) directionally, north, south, east or west. I'm not all that good at directions so if the sun's not shining I'm lost—so I ask or look it up or guess or something.

Naming the elevations directionally makes it less confusing if you need to explain where a particular damage is located. It's less confusing to say the left side of the east elevation, than to say the left side of the left side.

The first thing I do after getting out and gearing, up is walk to the best location to get a good overview of the front of the house. From there I begin all inspections—no matter what type of claim it is. Take a good front overview photo. And then, after taking the photo, I'll proceed to the front door to ring the doorbell.

NOTE: Even if the folks are standing in the driveway, chomping at the bit, tapping their foot, with their arms crossed staring holes in you...don't get in a hurry and skip taking the front overview photo first.

If you walk up to them and shake their hand, they'll start telling you about how the tree fell over in the backyard and crushed Susie's doll house and killed the dog. You'll follow them around the house and forget about the front overview. Wave, smile, holler, *hello,* but stay the course and walk to the best spot for a front overview and take the photo and then, meet and greet.

One day you won't, and then at night when you're loading the photos into your claim, you'll remember they got you side tracked. Also this is important because it keeps you in charge of the inspection. If you allow the insured or contractor to start dragging you around from spot to spot you'll have a hard time remembering and labeling your photos.

Do the same thing every time and whether it's a day claim or a hurricane—you're just running one at a time.

After I get the front photo, I meet the folks. We'll chat and I'll let them tell me their story. If you're working a storm claim, one that could affect the whole house, I'll hold my ground right there on the front driveway, as much as possible until they're done chatting.

Let them tell their story even though you've heard the same thing a hundred times already—they need to tell you. Let them. Make notes of anything they tell you that you weren't aware of from the loss report. Once introductions are done and they've had the chance to share their concerns, I'll launch into my opener. For example:

My job today is to take pictures and draw pictures. Usually, what I like to do, just out of habit, is start in the front and walk around clockwise, looking for anything that could be storm related. You're welcome to walk with me if you want, and if there's anything you want to show me feel free.

This relaxes the meeting and opens the door for the insured and or contractor to share all of their concerns. Don't hurry. You want to see and hear everything at the inspection, not in a phone call sometime later.

I start with a front overview photo and then any close up photos of damages located on the front elevation. I'll make notes of damages as I go.

For example:

_N_ (Indicating north elevation)

> *FACM8* (Noting the fascia metal 8" is damaged)

> *WW – 4* (Noting there are four damaged window wraps)

> *SDGV – MN* (Noting that the vinyl siding has minimal damage)

> *GUTA- 28* (Noting that 28' of the aluminum gutter system is damaged)

After I complete inspection for the front (or north elevation) I'll walk clockwise to the left (east) elevation to a spot where I can get a good overview photo of this elevation. And then I take close up photos of the damages and repeat the process around the house.

_E_ (Indicating East elevation)

> *WDA – PRIOR LWN MWR* Noting damage to aluminum window was preexisting- I'll write what caused the damage if I know. If I don't know, I'll put a question mark after it, and note accordingly in my report; (Preexisting damage from lawn mower or... appears to be preexisting damage, likely from lawn mower.)

NOTE: This process—overview photo followed by close ups of damage—is used in every situation for all claims. If you are working a water loss inside the home take an overview photo of the room, and then close ups of the damage. When you move to the next room first take an overview photo of the room, and then close ups of the damages. Make notes as you go under the heading for each location. Your notes should follow the order of your photos.

If you're documenting damage to the deck, take an overview photo of the deck and then close ups of the deck damage, if you're documenting damage to the fence, take an overview photo of the fence and then take close ups of the damage to the fence. And so on. Do this with all claims at all times and it will help you immensely when labeling your photos and following your notes.

As you work your way around the house make mental note of any other structures, like fences or other outbuildings, sheds etc. Don't detour to the other structures, stay on track and finish the main dwelling first.

Then, work your way down the scale as you would like to see it on your estimate. In other words; finish the house photos, and then move on to the detached garage, and then the shed and then the dog house and then the fence and then the personal property. Start big and work your way small. It'll be easier to write your report and your estimate when you've inspected in a systematic order.

If you're working a storm claim and they have a shed—inspect it. Even if they say it's not damaged.

Inspect and photo document it all. You don't want to get charged for another adjuster to go out and inspect the shed just because you thought, or the insured said, it wasn't damaged.

If they have interior damages I usually try to inspect them first, so I can get a feel for where the damage is located and I can pay special attention to any areas of concern on the exterior that may have resulted in the interior damage.

As much as possible stick to this inspection pattern: Coverage A, (main dwelling) and then inspect all of Coverage B (other structures) and then Coverage C (contents).

NOTE: Of course, it doesn't matter which way you walk around the house, clockwise or counter clockwise, the important thing is to get in a routine and do it the same way each time.

Take your time and look at anything that could be remotely related to the storm.

For example if you're working a hurricane and you notice a cracked window, take a picture of it first, and then ask about it. Even if you can tell the crack is old because it's faded and dirt filled—ask.

Make a note of why the window was damaged. Include the photo in your report with a note explaining that, as per insured it was preexisting damage from a separate event unrelated to claimed cause of loss; lawn mower threw a rock into the window. This will avoid monkey business on the back side of the claim when supplements and final payments are being requested.

Usually you're out of the picture by that time, but you'll look like a hero for going the extra mile and noting items that could become a potential issue.

What if you know the damage is old but the insured or contractor says it is storm related? Or the more common scenario:

How'd that window get cracked?

I don't remember seeing that before

So, you think it's from this storm?

Hmmm...I, I, uh, I don't know how that got there

This is where you get paid for being an adjuster. The task at hand is to tactfully win the confidence of the insured to acknowledge that the window was preexisting damage. ***ONLY if you know it was preexisting and even a blind man could see that it was preexisting***

If you're in doubt—give the benefit of the doubt to the insured. But, if you know that the damage is unrelated to the cause of loss you're inspecting, gently help the insured see why you think so. You may need to say nothing at first until you've won their confidence. You may need to leave it *lie* until later in the inspection, but you don't want to be coerced into telling the carrier that something was damaged from the storm when you know it wasn't, and you don't want to leave it unsettled. What I do in this situation is something like this:

Hmmm, so you're not sure how it got there huh? So, you think it's from the storm, maybe...I'll get real close and examine the cracked window and talk to myself loud enough to be heard...I don't know, this crack looks aged, faded, dirty...hmmm, I wonder if it could have been here for awhile it looks kind of...old.

Usually, they'll agree *Yeah, it was probably there before—I just don't remember seeing it.*

I'll tell them, *Yeah, it's hard to know sometimes because you never really look close at your house until after a storm and you're looking for damage. But, it's my job so I see all kinds of stuff and I figure it's best to ask.*

Again, you're letting the insured know that you're on their side, but you know what you're looking at and you aren't a push-over. If you agree to something that obviously isn't related damage, you may open a can of worms to remodel the entire house.

Sometimes, they'll hold their ground, wanting to get a new window (or whatever) out of the deal, or perhaps, they really don't know how it got damaged. Now, they've noticed it and want insurance to pay for it. You'll do well to listen close to your insured and address all their concerns, but at the end of the inspection you're going to let them know again, that your job is to take pictures and draw pictures. Tell them you'll relay all of their concerns and then give your recommendation to the carrier.

If you have an outstanding issue—such as the broken window—let them know that in your humble opinion you think the damage is unrelated, and tell them why you feel that way.

*Of course I didn't see the window before the
storm, so who am I to say what it looked like?
But, after looking at enough of them you get an
idea of what recent and old damage looks like,
and in my humble opinion it simply doesn't look
recent. The crack is faded and dirty and it's not
even located on the windward elevation (tell them
why you think it's not related). The window is
inches off the ground and reminds me of a crack
from a lawn mower throwing a stone. But that's
my opinion. I'll submit the picture for review.*

Assure them that all of their concerns will be
addressed. The worst thing you can do is make them feel
ignored. Address every concern, even if you know it's
trivial or unrelated. Sure, you could just blow them off
and forget about the stuff unrelated to the claim but *just
'cuz you can—don't mean you should.* If it's important to
the insured, it's important to the claim, even if it's
irrelevant it's relevant.

After you've finished the claim and have moved on
to another storm the thing you ignored will pop up and
bite you on the backside. It will look like you missed or
forgot something. And then, if your claim gets reopened
or re-inspected it could be viewed that you didn't do your
job. So, if the insured mentions it—you mention it. And it
can be as simple as saying:

*Insured said they didn't know how the east
elevation window got cracked—but it appears to
be preexisting, unrelated to claim. I explained this
to insured. See photo documentation.*

Remember

Do the same thing every time and whether it's a day claim or a hurricane—you're just running one at a time.

At times, even if it's irrelevant—it's relevant

Just 'cuz you can—don't mean you should

CHAPTER 7 ~ Diagrams & Measuring

If you are going to have to replace any siding; diagram and measure every elevation. I have my wife do that while I continue the inspection. For example if I'm looking at a hail claim, I'll finish my walk around and then get on the roof while my wife draws each elevation of siding. Saves time.

Why sketch the whole house if there's only a little damage on one elevation? Good question. Some states have matching laws that require the carrier to afford coverage to wrap the whole house if the siding is no longer available.

If you have all the measurements and draw them into your sketch program when you submit your initial report it will be easy and only take a few minutes to edit your claim to include all the siding if at a later date you are asked to do so.

If you don't have the measurements, and if you haven't included them in your initial report, you'll have to revisit the site or dig out your old notes—which in my case is too much work to dig through hundreds of field notes.

I just do it all up front, and then if I'm asked to wrap the house, I take a few minutes copy and paste the line items for siding into each elevation, change the billing (hopefully) to the new fee rate, and resubmit the claim. What would take over an hour to reconstruct takes me less than five minutes.

Pulling Samples

You may have to take a sample of siding to send to a laboratory to determine if a match is available. Normally the samples are sent to ITEL. (Go here for forms and information: http://www.itelinc.com/)

Pulling samples isn't fun but necessary at times. Never take a sample without the insured's approval and try to be considerate of the insured and take it from an inconspicuous location. One panel from nailing hem to bottom and about eight to twelve inches long is adequate. I always ask if they have a small sample, perhaps stored in the rafter of their garage. I explain why I need it, too. They may not want to tell you they have any spare pieces if they think you're going to tell them they can use those to make the repairs. So, explain why you want to know.

It doesn't matter if the sample is faded or not faded. Make sure you remove the siding from an area that you are going to recommend the carrier covers. For example if you are going to recommend coverage for the east elevation, then take your sample from the east elevation. If you take it from another elevation, that may commit the carrier to replacement of that side as well, because you damaged it. The sample is not returned to insured.

If I know I'm going to need to take a sample off the house and if a contractor is present, I'll ask them to get it for me. That way any liability falls to the contractor. If I have to remove it, I'll tape the area with duct tape to avoid water soaking the sheathing or house wrap. I know, it may not be necessary, but I like to err on the safe side. What if the work doesn't get completed for a long time and the sheathing deteriorates from exposure? If you cover it you'll be covering more than the hole, you'll be covering your butt, and you'll be going above and beyond most everyone else in the business.

NOTE: Pulling samples are dictated at the discretion of the particular carriers, but generally you will obtain samples of siding, roofing and or flooring if there is a question as to whether the item can be repaired or if it will need to be completely replaced due to matching complications.

Floor samples

When taking samples use common courtesy. I've heard adjusters brag about taking carpet samples out of the middle of the living room.

"Why?" I'd ask.

"So they have to replace it," they'd chuckle.

I don't get why that's funny. If you need a sample, take it from an inconspicuous location or from a spare piece they have left over. Use integrity and treat the insured with respect—like you'd like to be treated.

If you've got a wood floor that's slightly buckled from a water loss, I wouldn't rip up the floor to get a sample. If they have a spare piece—take one. Otherwise, I write the floor for a repair which consists of removing and replacing the obviously damaged portion and then I'll measure the entire wood floor and recommend refinishing all of it to match. Most of the time, this will give them enough money to do what they need to make proper repairs.

Many times a wood floor will dry and settle back into place. If you think this is a possibility, the proper repair methodology would be to dry, and refinish the surface. Many times you won't know for sure how the floor will turn out at the time you submit your estimate. Note this in your estimate and write for a repair first, but note that a supplement may be forthcoming if floor does not dry and settle back into place properly.

If carpet has been soiled with sewage or broken glass—replace it. The glass won't come out and if it's had black (sewer) water, it ought to be replaced. Your carrier may tell you otherwise but generally this is the best repair methodology. If the carpet was saturated with clean water, like a water line break, you can clean it for proper repairs but I always recommend the saturated portion of pad be removed and replaced.

Remember, if part of the floor has been damaged, and you're only going to write for a repair, you should still measure all the continuous run. If there is a natural break, such as a closing door with a threshold, or a break in the floor you can stop, but if the floor covering runs out of the kitchen and into the dining room and living room and entry way without any break in the floor; diagram and measure it all, even if the only damage was in front of the dishwasher.

Roof

Before you get off your ladder and onto the roof, stop. Take a photo of the pitch with your pitch gauge, a photo of the type shingle with your shingle gauge, a photo of how many layers, if ice and water shield is present and a photo of whether or not there is drip edge. Next, depending on the type of loss, I look at the gutter and fascia for damage.

Once I get on the roof I climb to the best spot to see an overview of the roof and take a roof overview. Then, if it's a hail claim, I'll mosey around the roof looking for collateral damage; things such as dents in soft metal vents, valleys etc. I'll look from the end of each ridge at the fascia and take a photo documenting damage or none. If I find dents on the east gable fascia I'll make a note of it under my east elevation notes. If it's safe to do so, I'll examine the gutters from the roof, too.

When inspecting the roof for hail or wind you will need to make a test square. Each carrier has their own idiosyncrasies but in general you'll need to draw a large letter indicating which slope you're on, such as a large N for north slope or a large S for south slope, E for east, W for west, some prefer to use a large F for front slope, B for back slope, R for right slope, L for left slope. Next to the letter you will draw a large equal sign (=).

Once you get your overview photo of the roof as a whole. You will take an overview photo of the slope and then circle the individual damages you find on that particular slope in a one square area. A square is a 10' x 10' area. Count how many circles you have in the square and write that number next to your equal sign. And then take an overview photo of the test square close enough so the number can be read in the photo. After that, take individual close up photos of each item you circled. This concludes your inspection of that particular slope. Repeat the process to each major slope.

NOTE: hail and wind damage to shingles is when the back weather proofing membrane is compromised. I tell folks if I could I'd press a button and flip every shingle over on the roof so I could just examine the back of the shingle—because, technically that's what I'm there to determine—did the back get damaged. Granule loss is not necessarily wind or hail damage but a wearable surface similar to the wear and tear of a vehicle tire.

Each carrier will tell you their number that constitutes a roof replacement verses repair.

Many times matching issues apply with shingles; in which case you may need to obtain a shingle sample to send off to determine availability. Make sure if you remove a shingle from insured's roof you put a temporary patch to avoid resultant interior leaking. If at all possible, I'll try to have insured's contractor remove the shingle.

The same philosophy holds true for roofs regarding diagramming. If you're going to recommend repair to any of it—measure all of it.

I've heard it a hundred times from folks in training. I don't want to measure this cotton-pickin' roof. It's a hundred degrees, the soles are melting off my boots. The roof is steep and big and more cut up than a sheet of paper at a scissor convention. Since we're only recommending one slope, do I have to measure and diagram the whole thing?

Yes.

Doggone it! I knew you'd say that.

I know it's old school. But I use a real tape measure and real paper and pencil and diagram and measure the whole cotton-pickin' thing—even if only part of the roof is damaged. I'm tempted not to. But, I regret it every time I fall prey to the contractor saying, "Hey, I'll have my guys measure it, and send you a copy."

The other temptation is to yield to the little green guys in outer-space that will send you a diagram from fifty-thousand miles in space. Actually, it's satellite imagery. This methodology has become quite popular and is used often. See CONTACTS for more information. For a fee you can order a diagram with all the measurements you need from one of these aerial imagery companies. I've used them at times when it was impossible to measure due to the extremity of damages or when it was very complex or too dangerous or inaccessible to measure accurately.

Satellite imagery is not infallible, however. I ordered a roof diagram for a large church complex that was obviously hundreds of squares. The roof had been blown almost completely off and covered with large blue tarps. The pitch of the roof made it virtually impossible to walk on the slippery tarps, so we ordered an aerial roof measurement from one of these companies. The fee was around seventy-five dollars. As it turned out I had to return to the site and painstakingly measure the roof the old fashioned way because the satellite imagery company had given me a nice diagram but the measurements were over a hundred squares short. Thankfully, it was such an obvious miscalculation that I knew to measure it myself rather than finding out after I had already submitted the claim. The company refunded my money.

On more than one occasion I've agreed to use an aerial imagery company on moss covered slippery steep complicated wood roofs and have been dismayed to find out they couldn't provide a measurement because of dense tree coverage. Resulting in a return visit to do what I should have done on my first visit. The technology increases by the day and now you can find out immediately from your smart phone if you can get an aerial measurement.

The technology is great and helps speed things along but it's important to know how to diagram and measure the loss manually incase these technologies are unavailable.

Another reason that it's a good idea to measure and diagram the roof yourself is that it forces you to do a thorough inspection; since you're all over the roof getting the measurements and drawing...plus it keeps one from getting lazy.

Denials

If you inspect the loss and can't find a cotton-pickin' thing wrong, or if the damage doesn't appear to be remotely related to the insured cause of loss. For example you get a wind claim where the insured claims wind damage to the roof shingles. When you inspect you find that the shingles are organic and curled from old age, but none are missing or have wind creases from being bent in the wind. You must still do due diligence prove that you did a thorough inspection. Actually, if I'm going to deny a claim, I take twice as many photos to prove I tried to find damage, and to document that it just wasn't there.

Any denial is likely to be challenged by a contractor or insured and you don't want them to say you were only on the roof for five minutes and you were in a hurry. Take your time, take a lot of pictures.

I explain to insured that in my humble opinion I couldn't see what looked like storm related damage. If the shingles are curled I explain that is a characteristic of aging organic shingles and has nothing to do with wind or hail. Hopefully a contractor is there and you can come to an agreement before you leave, otherwise you may see a re-inspect request in the near future. But if you show that you went above and beyond to find damage then no one will be able to say you missed something and shouldn't be paid for a return visit.

It's no secret that independent adjusters are paid on a sliding scale, so the higher the claim the higher the pay. This can be tactfully revealed to insured if you think they believe your job is to not find damage, and save the insurance company money.

Remember, more documentation is needed for no damage than when there is damage.

CHAPTER 8 ~ Inspection Review

Once you've completed your inspection it's important to wrap it up with a little chat. Your carrier may request you handle things differently. They may ask you to share nothing, but generally speaking you will do well to advise insured what you've found and what will take place next.

I'll summarize my findings by saying something like this:

> *Okay, I think we're done. What happens next is, I write my report with a recommendation. I say recommendation because that's what it is since it's not my checkbook. If it were my checkbook— I'd be fishing right now.*

The official phrase is: As an adjuster, I don't have authority to extend or deny coverage. But, no one remembers that. They do remember that you'd be fishing if it was your money. This will avoid a misunderstanding, where the insured or contractor states, "My adjuster said he was buying us a new roof." What if the claim gets rejected because the roof had already been paid for last year and the insured hadn't replaced it? What if the claim shouldn't have been sent to the field because the policy is expired? What if they disagree with your findings and don't want to cover the roof? Be safe and let the insured know that you don't make the final decision— it's not your checkbook.

Next summarize your findings:

And my recommendation is going to be that coverage is applied to the cost of replacing the roof since I found X amount of hits per square on your shingles.

For now I'll recommend replacement of the east elevation of siding and that may change depending on the ITEL report. That's why I measured and diagramed all the siding.

I'm going to recommend some miscellaneous items which you'll see on my estimate. Things like two aluminum window wraps on the east elevation and some fascia and gutters on that side, too.

I'll include photos of that one window we talked about—but I'm not sure how that'll go since it doesn't look like recent damage related to this storm. Remember, it looked to me like a lawn mower might have caused it. But, I'll include it for review and note your concerns.

The next question they'll ask will be: "What if there's not enough money." If they don't ask it, they'll be thinking it. So, go ahead and address the issue before they ask.

Now, I'll submit my report with labeled photos, diagrams, a summary of everything we've discussed and an itemized estimate, which you get a copy of so you can review and see how I came up with my totals.

If you want to you're welcome to share this with your contractor—I don't mind and there's nothing wrong with that. They may want to review it to make sure I didn't miss anything. Usually the contractor will complain that it's way too much money and you should send some of it back to the insurance company.

When you say that the contractor will start to faint; and the insured will get this deer-in-the-head-lights look. You'll have to snap them out of it. So, smile and tell them you're just kidding, but...

What happens if I missed something? Or what happens if you discover something that we didn't or couldn't notice today? That's not your fault. As long as it's legitimate, a supplement can be requested. That means requesting additional funds because—we found an additional layer of shingles we couldn't see until removal had begun...or part of the house had plank sheathing and needs to be re-decked...or we found more damage to another window wrap or...whatever.

As long as it's legitimate.

We can't allow contractors to hijack the market just because it's insurance—and they have a yacht payment due. So, what I usually do if a supplement is requested is say: 'repeat after me...this is an insurance claim...not a poker hand.' Then, I'll ask the contractor to document with an itemized estimate that details exactly what, and how much they are asking for, and why. Usually—as long as it's legitimate—this will suffice. But, what's important is that this is not poker. You can't just pick out the cards you like and discard the ones you don't. If the bottom line is enough then semantics don't matter. For example; if it'll cost ten grand to replace the roof and my estimate is for ten grand then it doesn't matter if your contractor says I don't have enough ice and water shield or valley metal or whatever. If there's enough money at the bottom of the page then the line items above don't matter. In other words—no cherry-pickin' allowed.

Oh, and one more thing—if you think there's something that needs to be supplemented, you can still cash the check. I've heard folks tell me they're not going to cash the check because they don't agree with the amount. I don't know where that came from. Go ahead and cash the check—put it in the bank—it doesn't mean you're signing off as if it's a done deal. Your carrier wants to do what's right and settle the claim for what's due.

I know it sounds like I'm stating the obvious, but you'll save yourself hours of file reviews if you set the stage up front, that greed won't be tolerated. It gets strange at the end of a storm when the claims start to slow down. Suddenly you'll see a bunch of claims kicking back requesting little things; a couple hundred dollars here and a thousand there, just to bump the claim a little higher. Contractors get time on their hands and the new jobs start to slow down and a bird in the hand is worth... So, they'll start trying to generate more income by adding a little fat to the jobs they've already got. Can't hardly blame them, can you?

You'll do well to develop a rapport with the insured and contractor that encourages a spirit of moral integrity and cooperation to settle the claim for a reasonable cost of repair and move on.

Time line

Once you address the money issue the next thing on their mind is: How soon is it going to get here? I'll say something like this:

> Alright, typically what happens next is—within a day or so I write up my recommendation and submit it for review. If all goes well the file is reviewed within a few days and submitted recommending payment. And then a copy of my report and a check is printed and mailed. So, giving me a couple days, them a couple days and the printing and check writing and mail time I'd say in about ten days to two weeks you should see something in the mail.
>
> Now, you may get two separate mailings. My report may come in the mail one day and then a few days later you may get a check—or visa-versa. They used to send them together in one envelope but they feel sorry for the post-office since everybody uses email instead of snail mail nowadays, so they wanted to help them out by spending more money on postage.

That's not really the reason, but it's one that the insured will remember and keep you and the office from getting a hundred calls claiming the check was forgotten. The real reason is that some carriers have separate divisions; one handles check writing and another handles file reviews, thus they are mailed from separate places.

So your goal was to give them a time line of ten days to two weeks before they start calling. Much of the time, if you get your report in within a day or two, they'll get their report before the ten day mark. You may get specific instructions from your carrier as to what time line to expect or share with the insured. Some carriers may tell you not to give them a timeline at all.

Expect some folks to start calling on day ten asking, "Where's my money." Don't worry it's just human nature.

You're almost done.

Deductible and depreciation (hold back)

Let me explain how the payments work. Let's say I write your report and it's reviewed and they agree with the total I came up with on my estimate. They will take the grand total and deduct your deductible. That's easy to remember right? Your deductible is deducted.

Next, even on a replacement cost policy, they hold back a certain amount for the material cost of items being replaced, not labor. The percentage held back is calculated according to the age and condition of the material. It's called depreciation—but I think a better name for it is 'hold back'. Because on a replacement cost policy that's really what it is—just held back until the work is done.

If they start to squirm, cross their arms and get this just-bit-a-lemon look. You'll need to explain a little more.

For example for easy math let's say your total claim is for your roof and cost ten grand to replace. Let's say your deductible is five hundred bucks. That leaves ninety-five hundred dollars, right? Now let's say there is a thousand dollars depreciation—or hold back. That leaves eighty-five hundred bucks, right? So, in this situation an initial check is sent to you for eighty-five hundred bucks. Now, once you complete the work, usually your contractor handles this part, because they want to get paid. What I used to do when I was a contractor was make a 'Certificate of Completion' and I'd advise the carrier via fax that the work on claim number such and such for so and so had been completed please release all 'hold back'.

So, in other words, when the work is done you or your contractor will submit documentation, such as a final invoice for the amount agreed upon, which in this case is ten thousand dollars. And the carrier will in turn release the held back depreciation which in our example is one thousand bucks. So when all is said and done and you've completed all the repairs you would have received the total, less your deductible; or, in this example, ninety-five hundred dollars.

On the other hand, if you decide to take the initial eighty-five hundred bucks and buy a bass boat— well then, the hold back is never released—and I hope the fish are biting.

After I say the 'bass boat' part it usually clicks and the light comes on. Now, you should understand that the above is a simplified version of what takes place. The depreciation is also set in place, in case the insured gets the work done for cheaper than the amount stated in the loss report; in which case the depreciation is adjusted accordingly and the final payout matches the actual cost incurred less the deductible. You may need to explain that as well if they press the issue thinking they may do the work themselves or have Uncle Bob do it for a case of beer and a burger.

Technically, insured are not to profit from an insurance claim. On the surface money is the issue. How much do I get and how fast can I get it. But, the real meat of an insurance contract is a good-faith agreement. Both parties must behave in the spirit of good-faith for the process to proceed as it is designed.

You are the instrument to facilitate this process. Therefore, money is not the biggest issue in an insurance claim. The mechanics of adjusting may be crunching numbers but the heart of an adjuster is helping people who've suffered a loss be made whole in the most respectful equitable fashion. And that doesn't just mean monetarily. Sometimes your greatest gift to the insured is to be there and let them tell you their story. Which brings us to the heart of adjusting.

CHAPTER 9 ~ Ethics

Insurance; the only thing you have to buy and hope you never use.

The contract of insurance is a moral contract. The carrier agrees to take monies from an individual in return for nothing—but a promise; a promise of coverage in the event of a covered loss. Both parties agree to act in good faith toward one another. The insured agrees to act in good faith by acting with reasonable care to protect property insured against. And the insurance carrier agrees to apply coverage in a timely and equitable fashion in the event of a loss.

All of the above is tied together with a cord of trust. One party trusting the other, when the cord is broken, the whole thing comes undone. The job of the adjuster during the claims process is to keep that cord of trust unbroken.

It is not the adjuster's job to save the insurance company money, as is the common belief in many circles on both sides of the fence—carrier and insured alike. The adjuster's job is to determine coverage, document and present the claim and negotiate a settlement. Or, at least recommend a settlement. Sometimes the carrier will dictate that the settlement process be left to their inside claims handlers.

It may go without saying but an adjuster should be careful not to get involved with any conflicts of interest such as working as a contractor and an insurance adjuster or receiving any compensation regarding an insurance claim other than that which is provided via the carrier they are representing.

I recently finished my continuing education requirements for my Florida adjusters' license; included in the studies was the Florida code of ethics. I'm not sure all states have similar codes, but whether they do on don't, you'd do well to follow this code.

Code of Ethics

Florida Adjusters Code of Ethics

1.   An adjuster must put fair and honest treatment of the claimant above their own interests;

2.   An adjuster cannot steer any claimant needing repairs or other services to any person with whom the adjuster has an undisclosed financial interest or who is anticipated to provide the adjuster with any compensation for the referral for any resulting business;

3.   An adjuster should not provide any favored treatment to any claimant;

4. An adjuster must adjust claims strictly in accordance with the insurance contract;

5. An adjuster must not approach investigations, adjustments, and settlements in a manner prejudicial to the insured;

6. An adjuster must make truthful and unbiased reports of the facts making a complete investigation;

7. An adjuster must act with dispatch and due diligence in achieving a proper disposition of the claim;

8. An adjuster must report to the Department any conduct by a licensed insurance representative of this state which violates any provision of the Insurance Code or Department rule or order;

9. An adjuster must exercise extraordinary care when dealing with elderly clients to make sure they are not disadvantaged by failing memory or impaired cognitive processes;

10. An adjuster cannot negotiate with a third-party represented by an attorney, if he has knowledge of the attorney. This does not apply to an insured or the insured's resident relatives;

11.   An adjuster is permitted to interview any witness without the consent of the opposing counsel or party. However, the adjuster must avoid any suggestion calculated to induce a witness to suppress or deviate from the truth. If the witness gives a signed or recorded statement and requests a copy the adjuster must provide a copy;

12.   An adjuster cannot advise a claimant to refrain from seeking legal advice or retaining legal counsel;

13.   An adjuster cannot negotiate with or obtain a statement from a claimant or witness at a time they would reasonably be expected to be, in shock or serious mental or emotional distress as a result of physical, mental, or emotional trauma associated with a loss;

14.   An adjuster cannot conclude a settlement when the settlement would be disadvantageous to a claimant who has been traumatized or distressed by a loss;

15.   An adjuster cannot give legal advice;

16.   An adjuster must be competent and knowledgeable as to the terms and conditions of the insurance coverage

CHAPTER 10 ~ Policy Language

In my humble simplified opinion, and if you keep a little flexibility, an insured claim can be whittled down to three words:

Sudden. Accidental. Loss.

Sudden: It happened from an event, not a long term process such as, fading from the sun, or the twenty year old unfinished deck dry-rotted until the railing fell over.

Accidental: You didn't drive your car through the back wall of the garage on purpose.

Loss: There's got to be a loss, to be a loss. Smart, huh? Old chipped, peeling paint that has a few marks from hail does not constitute a loss. If it hasn't been damaged functionally, physically, cosmetically or monetarily—then it's not damaged. And thus, no loss has been suffered. Evidence of an insured peril doesn't necessarily mean a loss has been suffered. It goes back to good old fashioned common sense.

If the event was sudden, accidental and an actual loss occurred in most cases it is covered. Of course you'll want to read policy language regarding exclusions. For example: surface water running into the house could be sudden, accidental and a loss may occur, but surface water is an exclusion, in typical policy language. Nevertheless, with the exception of the basic exclusions, you can use those three words, *sudden accidental, loss* as a general rule of thumb as to whether an event is covered or not.

Policy language can be confusing for everyone—especially the insured. It's important to remember that the policy is interpreted in favor of coverage in the event of ambiguity. I like to say:

If in doubt—err in favor of the insured

CHAPTER 11 ~ Claim Writing

No matter which program your carrier requests, your loss report package will contain five things. You'll need to tell them what happened five ways—according to their particular idiosyncrasies.

1. Tell them with words
2. Tell them with photos
3. Tell them with diagrams
4. Tell them with an estimate
5. Tell them with your bill $:-)

Telling them with words usually called your *short form* or *general loss report*. Basically it's a summary of the loss, your recommendation for repairs and a note of any issues (like prior damage from a separate event.) Try to be courteous and professional. This is not the place to say, "The insured was a fat jerk, the contractor is an idiot and the public adjuster oughta be shot...Besides that, their dog is ugly." It may be true, and there may be a place to say those things—but I don't know where.

Tell them with photos is a list of all your pictures and you must label each one explaining where and what the photo depicts. I usually arrange mine in the order my estimate follows. Overviews then close ups of damage. I'll delete photos that are duplicates or not of good quality. I'll group my items together, like all of the roof, all the siding, all the gutters...etc. You want to show and tell them the story with your pictures.

Tell them with diagrams is a way to point out where specific damages occurred and document the quantities you used in your estimate. Good drawings make for a first class loss report. When you first start learning various adjuster programs I recommend you invest time in the sketch portion learning how to diagram effectively. It'll pay off in time and money in the long run.

Tell them with the estimate shows how you came up with the dollar figure you're recommending. Take your time and make this as professional looking as possible. Write it in an order that makes sense.

For example, if you're replacing the roof start with removal and then replacement of the various items just like it would occur during construction. If you're repairing some drywall and replacing carpet start at the top and work your way down like you'd do it in real life. For example: Repair the drywall, the insulation and paint the wall, then replace the carpet and the baseboard. Make it make sense. The person reviewing your file is already googly-eyed from reading estimates.

Make yours easy to understand and it will pass inspection quicker and get you paid. Plus, it'll make you a favorite to receive new claims. Speaking of which...

Payday

After working a storm for a little while I heard an adjuster say, *soon the money will start flowing like water*. You wouldn't mind that would you?

Most companies will set up automatic payments directly into your bank account and they usually pay twice a month. If you don't have direct deposit you can ask your bank directly if they will deposit your checks if they're mailed to them. And then ask your accounting department if they'll mail your checks to the bank address—I call it my redneck direct deposit system. I've done it that way when I was on the road and direct deposit wasn't offered.

Also, I have all my bills set up to auto-pay. You'll get so busy *turnin' & burnin'* that you'll forget what day of the month it is. If you're working a hurricane a thousand miles from home you won't want to mess with your mail.

Setting everything on autopilot will make your life simpler and make for a more harmonious *Adjuster's Life*.

CHAPTER 12 ~ Tools

Compass: What's the first thing you do when you get to the right place? Write F=____. A compass will help.

GPS: I've been known to say, "If we didn't get lost at least once a day—it meant we never left the hotel." I can still get lost but a good GPS helps and it'll pay for itself in the time you'll save.

Tool belt: I use a CatManDo adjusters tool belt. It works great for carrying a clip board and camera, and all your other tools www.customtoolbelt.com is one place that carries it. It's around a hundred bucks and will last for years.

Digital camera: I've used a Sony Cyber-Shot for years. I bounced it down valleys, off roofs, dropped it in gutters and it still clicked. Finally, after watching it bump and grind down a steep metal valley and grand slam into the gutter I noticed the battery door didn't shut quite right. So, I did what any redneck MacGyver would do. I duct taped it. Worked fine—looked stupid. So, I went in search of a new camera. They're all light weight junk these days and I couldn't find one with a rear view-finder. So, I went on e-bay and bought every eight to ten-year-old Sony Cyber-Shot I could find. Only paid about twenty bucks a piece and it's a mighty fine tough little camera. Do you best to find one with a rear view finder you look through, most have the LCD screens only, which is awful to see what you're taking a picture of in the sunlight. What's important in a camera is not how great a picture—you only need about 5 megapixels. You want one with the ability to dial down the photos to e-mail size (like 640x480) so you can load them in programs without wasting time resizing; a flash that you can turn on and off manually. If the flash is always on in low light you'll have trouble capturing some water marks on white drywall—it'll look like you're camera went snow-blind. A zoom is nice up to 5 X or so; a memory stick that will hold about 300 pictures and will slip out and into your laptop; and rechargeable batteries will save you a fortune.

Chalk: I use soap stone. It's cheap and it doesn't make a mess. You can find it by the metal working stuff like welding supplies etc.

Pitch gauge: A gizmo that tells how steep the roof is, we used to just use our ankles to know if it was steep, but now most carriers want a picture of it. You can find these where roofing supplies are sold—and of course nowadays...there's an app for that, on your smart phone.

Shingle gauge: Made by Haag engineering and can be ordered wherever roofing supplies are sold. Again, we used to just know by looking at the shingle what it was. But nowadays most carriers require a photo of the gauge on the shingle to determine. Off the record, I gave my first one away to someone I was training in. Said it made a good shoe-horn but that was about it. When word came out that we had to take a photo depicting the gauge of the shingle—I refused. Said the gauge isn't accurate, but finally, I was told it wasn't an option, use the gauge or lose the claim. So, I'm taking pictures of the shoe-horn with every claim now, (remember, that was off the record).

Water meter: This will help you measure moisture content in surfaces during a water loss. If you have one that lights up you'll be glad you can turn the flash off on your camera when you take a picture of your reading. These are sold in home supply stores.

Laser tape: This will save time measuring interiors. Rather than snaking your tape measure around the sofa, rocker and piano. Just stand in the corner and click one way then the other and you're done.

Tape measure: I always use a 35' tape as stiff as I can find. Fat Max makes a good one.

Duct tape: You know—for your camera. No, I use it to cover exposures after taking a siding sample...been tempted to use it on a mouth or two, but didn't.

Siding zip tool: Handy little tool like a bent can opener to help remove and replace vinyl siding.

Cougar Paws (Spider man boots): Roofing supply stores sell boot that are made for walking on roofs. The sole is held on with Velcro and it's real soft, which is good so you don't slip on the steep ones but bad because since it's real soft it wears out quick. The boots will run about $150 and the replacement soles about $15.00. Only wear these on steep roofs to save your sole.

Gloves: Shingles can get hot enough to fry an egg and remove your fingerprints if you're not careful. I just use good old fashioned leather, snug fit so I can still write and operate the camera with them on. A lot of folks use the mechanics gloves. Those work good, too—but I've found the leather ones are cheaper and they last longer.

Rechargeable batteries: I've found that AA is pretty common in the stuff I need. I use them in my flashlight, my camera and some other electronic gadgetry.

Flashlight: I use a small one that uses rechargeable AA batteries and it fits in my tool pouch.

Mechanical pencils: The first time you try to write in the cold with an ink pen you'll understand why.

Checkered (graph) paper: I'll use this because it helps with diagramming.

Clip board: The metal kind you see in truck stops is what I've used for years. I clip my current claim to the top—if it rains it has a flap to cover the paper. And when I'm done it opens and has a place to store the completed files. At the end of the day all my field notes are right there handy in one place. It fits in the side pouch of my tool bag perfectly.

Hat: This is up to you, but looking up on sunny days it sure is nice to have a little shade for the eyes.

Cell phone: Smart phones have the capability to be used as a pitch gauge, a compass, a GPS, a day-timer, an alarm clock, some can even interface with adjuster program software and satellite imageries...and believe it or not, a few adjusters even use them to make phone calls.

CHAPTER 13 ~ Websites & geeky stuff like that

Weather sites to obtain date and area specific weather reports sometimes documentation is requested by carrier:

www.noaa.gov

www.wunderground.com

www.weather.com

Websites to socialize with other adjusters and post your resume:

www.catadjuster.org – Post your resume on this site and check often for venders looking for adjusters

www.adjusterspace.org A social network site for adjusters. Jobs are here too.

www.adjusterpro.com Blog featuring commonly asked questions for adjusters.

www.claims-portal.com

Adjuster programs

www.xactware.com Xactimate software and training

www.simsol.com   Simsol software and training

www.powerclaim.com Power Claim software and training

www.msbinfo.com   MSB/Integra Claims software and training

NOTE: I'd go to each of these sites and contact them about receiving a trial program. Some will give it to you for free for thirty days. For sure contact Xactimate and even if you need to buy the program for a month—it's a good idea to get it in your hands and get familiar with it. Play with it. And remember, with each one you handle, add in your resume something like: Experience with: Xactimate, Simsol, Powerclaim, MSB.

Computer software needed

www.pdffactory.com Opens and saves PDF files and faxes.

www.excel.com Microsoft Office includes Excel but it's needed to open numerous insurance documents and forms

www.efax.com Receive and send faxes like e-mails. Get your own fax number. Print without a printer from hotel room.

www.microsoftword.com Needed for writing reports

Venders to send your resume to

www.icaadjusters.com I've worked over a decade with this outfit and they've kept me plenty busy. Tell them you read my book and I sent you.

www.pilotcat.com

www.worleyco.com

www.eberls.com

www.uscatadj.com

There are many more. Check out www.catadjuster.org and get on every roster you can until you get settled in the saddle with the one or few you like.

Other useful links

www.itelinc.com (order sample forms etc.)

www.adjusterpro.com

www.claimspages.com

www.claimsresourcedir.org

www.insurancetech.com

www.claims.com

www.naic.org (NAIC State Licensing Page)

www.sircon.com

CHAPTER 14 ~ Dougisms

- *Take yer time you'll get there faster*

- *I'm here to take pictures and draw pictures*

- *They're all easy—some just take longer than others*

- *If there was no such thing as insurance— would you throw it out?*

- *It's not my check book, so your carrier will make the final decision. If it were my check book...I'd be fishing right now.*

- *What's a reasonable cost of repairs?—Pretend you're paying for it*

- *Just cuz you can—don't mean you should*

- *If it's important to the insured, it's important to the claim, even if it's irrelevant it's relevant*

Things I've learned as an adjuster

- _If the slope of the roof is just right a digital camera can bounce clean over a four-foot picket fence._
- _If the slope of the driveway is just right, you can back a ladder clean through an overhead garage door window._
- _A tape measure sliding off the roof makes the same kind of dent on the hood of my pick up as it does to a Mercedes Benz—just cost more to fix the Benz._
- _After scaling Mount Everest 10/12, three-story, it's the wrong time to realize you forgot to charge the camera batteries_
- _Shauna Lane isn't the same thing as Shauna Street_

Conclusion

Thank you for your time. I've enjoyed it and consider it an honor. Now, I pray you'll have a safe and prosperous, *Adjuster's Life*.

Remember you're in the people business and it's not what you do for a living that matters, it's who you are. And nobody can be you, as good as you. So, the way I see it, *that* makes you world champion You-nique.

Let me know if there's anything I can do to help.

God bless & be safe

Doug Spurling

Dougspurling@aol.com

www.ingramcontent.com/pod-product-compliance
Lightning Source LLC
Chambersburg PA
CBHW071606170526
45166CB00003B/1010